'Still Crazy'

Barney S. Smith

Produced and Published by Dennis Barber Ltd.

5 Battery Green Road
Lowestoft
Suffolk
NR32 1DE

ISBN 0-9553674-0-9
ISBN 978-0-9553674-0-3

Design and layout by Evan Carr, Dennis Barber Ltd.

This is dedicated to all those I have ever Loved

I still love them

No regrets

No explanations

Acknowledgements

A tremendous "Thank You" to Linda, Dennis and Evan and all those who work for and with them at Dennis Barber Ltd.

Without Linda's encouragement and determination this would never have reached print.

Many, Many Thanks.

There are many others, you know who you are.
You have my thanks and my love.

Contents

Awakening

The robin filled the air with song as I awoke this morning
A herald were those strident notes, that another day was dawning.
As I stretched and yawned and laid, there, just listening to his song.
An answering call came floating back and it wasn't very long.
Before other birds, with other notes, joined in the morning chorus
As if to tell the waking world, there's another day before us.
The blackbird, thrush and starling soon took up the round.
The wren, the tit, the chaffinch enhanced the choral sound.
Their clear, melodious voices in sweetest harmony blended
And then! as if by some command, their symphony was ended.
The world was silent, not a sound, as if with breath drawn in
Each waited for the clamorous noise of a new day to begin.
Then, one by one their praises sung, they went upon their way.
Their task was done, they had roused the world to a great, big, brand new day.

Bye-bye Blackbird

Today I have witnessed quite a rare sight,
Something too many men have not seen.
A mother protecting her babies with love
In a home that was soft warm and clean.

The rain tumbled down on their roofless retreat.
She gathered her chicks to her breast.
Six tiny babies that needed to eat
And to stay soft and warm in the nest.

How cruel men are. ~ He wasn't around.
He had just flown off for the day.
She called ,no response, he couldn't be found
He was off on his old round allay.

She twittered and fluttered to all no avail.
She thought this is really absurd.
A few words were clear from those that she uttered,
"He's flown off with some other bird."

Barney S. Smith

Home

The flat lands of East Anglia have a beauty all their own
And the poets and the painters have made it quite well known.
When you stand and gaze around you, there's no need to wonder why
You catch your breath and marvel at the vastness of the sky.

The flatlands stretch for miles and miles so that everyone can see,
The shimmering silken colours of natures tapestry.
No distant hill to beckon or to dominate the scene.
Just the blue and gold of summer and the luscious verdant green.

The swifts and swallows overhead can't fail to catch the eye,
As they dive and dart and winnow in a cloudless, clear blue sky.
The golden corn lies gleaming like a pirate's treasure hoard.
The scene is such one can't forget the marshland and the broad.

Jenkins Crag Windermere

The sky has cleared and filled with light
To reveal again a familiar sight.
Familiar, yes, but not the same.
For once again the patterns change.
The sparkle of sun on the lake below
That wasn't there a moment ago.
A seagull wheeling in the breeze
Soon hidden from sight amongst the trees.
The tip of a mountain enveloped in cloud.
Shows hazily through a misty shroud.
Just a moment in time ~ but tomorrow I'll say,
"It looks just the same as yesterday."

Puddleduck

A duck sat in a puddle. his face creased in a frown.
He really felt quite silly in a puddle on his own.
He could been with Ida, she'd said she'd meet him in the town,
But like the silly duck he was he'd just turned Ida down

He thought he was quite handsome and it seemed to him absurd
That with his snow white feathers, he could not attract some other bird.
He preened his feathers once again and made a quick inspection.
Could that muddy thing that looked at him be really his reflection?
He splashed the puddle once again then quacked, "I'm out of luck.
I'm not the handsome bird I thought I was.I'm just a silly, puddle duck.".

Peter and Life

"Life, is a puzzle" said Peter.
"Not so", said his quizzical friend.
"If you are farthest from the beginning.
You must be nearest the end."

"Why do what we do?" asked Peter.
"It all seems to be no avail"
'Not so', said the masterly mentor.
"For if we don't try, we can't fail."

"Should I then be happy?" asked Peter.
"With a permanent smile on my face?"
"If you are wearing a smile," said his mentor.
"Then that would be the right place."

Asked Peter, "What might happen
If day became night and night day?"
Said the mentor, "We'd either be late or be early,
But I'm sure we'd live the same way."

"Will you always be with me?" asked Peter,
"Or will you some day disappear?"
"I'm your spirit and conscience," said mentor,
"And you know I will always be here."

October Reverie

For me October seems to be ,
The month that charts my destiny;
The month in which I first drew breath;
The month in which I first saw death;

The month my mother gave me life ;
The month I took myself a wife.
And every year this same month brings
Sweeping changes in many things.

The hedgerows show their autumn tints,
And there are many other hints
Of winters sleep, and summers ending
And broken friendships that need mending.

For October signifies to me,
A hidden sense of urgency.
Not to leave all things to fate
But get them done ere it's too late.

A reminder to do all I can,
To live well with my fellow man.
And many things, these are but few,
What does October mean to you?

Where Is My Hedgehog

Where is my hedgehog? Where is she gone?
Where on earth can she be?
I've looked all over, but I cannot find her
Has she run away from me?

Where is my hedgehog? Why is she missing?
Has she gone off on her own?
I'm sure she is lonely ,I'm sure she is wishing
She was safely back home.

Where is my hedgehog? She knows that I love her,
If you see her please say that I care.
I want her to linger, whilst I run my finger.
Through her prickly hedgehog hair.

Are! here is my hedgehog ,or can I see doubles?
I wish I clearly could see,
For it looks like my hedgehog has turned into bubbles,
Oh dear! Oh! Oh! deary me!

But it doesn't matter, because I still love her
And if you look closely you'll see
Although she tries hard too, she can't put a stop too,
The feelings she feels about me.

Barney S. Smith

The Outing

Chattering housewives on an outing for the day,
Great excitement at the chance to get away.
The clattering of the train wheels going round,
Poor competition for the noisy sound.
For each have their own news to relay
And after all they've only got the day.

In time with speeding train their speedy word
For each of them is anxious to be heard.
How's Charlie? Oh, he's fine. And what of Fred?
Oh him, I've left the lazy blighter still in bed.

Ah Jane, I hear that you've become an auntie yet once more
How many does that make now? ~Three or four?
You've brought some photographs of baby Jim.
Hm! not a bit like her but more like him.

Oh Sue, you really have to tell us more
About the goings on of them next door.
Is it true that really "she's" a man?
How can you tell the difference? If you can
And can you really say that they're all right
And don't you worry when you're in your bed at night?

You'll never guess who I had on the phone.
She rang me up to say she's on her own.
No! not Elizabeth, but mousy Joyce,
You know, the one who's got the gravely voice.

The Outing cont...

Well, it seems her husband Peter's had enough
And has gone off with another piece of stuff.

Oh what about the dinner dance the other night?
A few of them there really looked a sight!
And didn't Mary whatsit look a mess
Parading in that off the shoulder dress?
And did you see Belinda Mayhew there?
I hardly recognised her with that frizzy hair.

That Ben and Rita , did you hear them shout,
I would not be surprised he's knocking her about.
Now:- shall we decide what we will do this afternoon,
For we will be arriving at the station soon?
Well here we are, come on Sue don't lag
Wake up Jane ! and don't forget your bag.!

Barney S. Smith

The Loving Cup

The loving cup or loving bowl,
Is pure reflection of the soul.
And if by chance you over fill it
As sure as fate some day you'll spill it!

Difference Twixt Loving

The difference twixt loving and being in love
Are aeons and aeons apart.
The basis of each is a warm glowing feeling,
Spontaneous straight from the heart.

And loving is caring with the need to protect
A feeling that many can share.
A sheltering harbour of comfort and warmth
And the knowing twill always be there.

But being in love is a much harder game;
A feeling beyond our control.
The needing, the loving, the pleasure, the pain.
Not caring for selling ones soul.

Destroying all logic affecting the brain
Sense to insensibility turns.
The uncontrollable feeling of going insane,
While loves passion rages and burns.

No respector of persons, class, colour or creed
This awesome emotion arrives
With a clear indication of showing us where
We could be fulfilling our lives.

It's then that the loving and being in love,
Dictate the path that we chose.
For it might be in keeping the ones that we love
The one we're in love with, we lose.

For life is a conflict, no answer is clear
There is no earthly way to dictate,
Those we fall in love with or those we just love;
The whole thing is governed by fate.

Barney S. Smith

Points Of View

I've searched in vain but have not found
Encouragement to make a sound.
To shout out loud the way I feel
To make men notice my ideal.
Though insignificant I am ,
I bleed the same as any man.
And if just once the world could see
There is some usefulness in me;
Someone may hear my plaintiff cry
And discover when I die
Some reason to my point of view.
The misery that I went through.
The agony it took to say,
The chosen words I use today.
So passion spent I must remain
The inarticulate again.

Imagination

Waiting for inspiration,
Seeking a way to find.
The path to imagination,
The key to a shuttered mind.

The road to everyone's freedom
That an open mind will allow;
Make believe and day dreaming
Are just ways of showing us how.

Of showing us how to remember
The things in life we've enjoyed.
Showing us how to find pleasure
By imagination fully employed.

Just lie back and let your thoughts wander.
Go with them wherever they go.
Just open your mind to adventure
And wonderful things you don't know.

Just have faith in yourself it can happen
And it has for those who have tried;
For they have summoned the magic
And found a new world deep inside.

It is there for the rich and the poor ones.
It is there for both young and old.
No matter for health or shortage of wealth.
We must open our mind and be bold.

Barney S. Smith

Imagination cont...

For we have seen the smiles of the children
As they play in their own wonderland.
Transported as if by magic
To a place that they understand.

And the tender glance of the lover
As he looks in his loved ones eyes.
He sees his answers are in there
And they take him to paradise.

For isn't it dreams that inspire us?
That begs us to stand up and shout.
Open your mind, for in there you'll find,
Just what living is really about.

For who would want the life of the closed ones?
The one's who really can't see;
That life is not about being shackled,
But having the right to be free.

And it is our dreams that inspire us,
The secret thoughts we hold in our head.
And some of our dreams inspire others;
Some dreams live even after we're dead.

The Dove And The Butterfly

And granddad will be a butterfly when he stops being a man.
And he will come to visit you each summer if he can.
And I'm sure that you will know him, as he dances through the air.
You will see him unexpectedly, for like magic he'll be there.
And granddad will be a butterfly.

And granddad will be a butterfly when his time as a man is done;
So we can go on playing games and having lots of fun.
He'll flit through the air above your head and much to your surprise ~
Now you'll see him, now you won't. He'll disappear before your eyes.
And granddad will be a butterfly.

And granddad will be a butterfly and grandma will be a dove.
And she will teach you many things of nature and of love.
She'll teach you just which bird sings what and what their colours are.
And how their shapes are different when you see them from afar.
And grandma will be a dove.

And grandma will teach you many things of all that you are fond.
Of the flowers in the garden, and the strange world in a pond.
And granddad will be a butterfly and grandma will be a dove;
And with the help of mum and dad, they will fill your hearts with love.
And granddad will be a butterfly.
And grandma will be a dove.

for mother with love.

Permission To Leave

The shadow of the reaper flits quietly across the wall;
A soft and silent sentinel waiting for the call
To take you gently in his arms and carry you to rest;
To a land that's warm and loving filled with things that you know best.
No need to struggle any more, to endure the earthly pain
For love and beauty flourish there, on that great ethereal plane.
The home of loved ones long since gone, of family and friends.
All of them are gathered there to greet you once again.
No time for tears or sadness now for those you'll leave behind;
You know that they 'll be joining you in the fullness of their time.
So make the journey now my love: just take the reapers hand.
Go find the peace that you deserve in knowing I understand.

Borrowed Time

Why is there such sweet sadness at the passing of each day?
The urge to catch each passing hour : and hold it there to stay.
The knowledge that as time goes by, the minutes and the seconds;
The hand of time just reaches out, and with 'it's' finger beckons.
The aged face with knowing smile, looks at the work begun.
He nods his head as if to say 'The span of life is one'
No second chance to get it right, you have to do it now.
And so dear friend, we struggle on the tiresome path somehow
And 'though the burden's heavy, we share the load my friend.
And somehow we'll be together, when we reach our journey's end.

An Invitation To Dance

I hold my breath and wait entranced,
At the thought of inviting myself to the dance
In time with the music. My minds in a whirl
At the thought of me joined in a twist and a twirl.

I stand by the river and look at the trees
And notice the dance of the leaves on the breeze.
I raise my sights higher to look to the sky.
To see formation of clouds as they go dancing by.

And, in the warm evenings, when the weather is fair,
Gnats in high rhythm dance on the air.
Dancing sunlight on water dazzles the eye,
As down to the sea the rivers dance by.

Dancing like dervishes, the whole human race
Goes dancing by at a hell of a pace.
And will I be able , I ask, if perchance;
I let go of my fears to join in the dance.

And will I say no, or will I say yes?
The answer I fear is anyones guess.
It seems life is calling come take a chance.
Come join the rest of life in the dance.

Ode To A Rose

Oh rose, sweet rose, in awe I gaze on thee;
Thy royal splendour nature has endowed so bounteously,
Your brilliant lustre to enhance lifes tapestry.

A hidden strength within thy thorny stem there lies
Majestic power, to hold your beauty to the skies
For adulation, and for worship from adoring eyes.

As courtiers in attendance, the leaves dark green
Are cast in symmetry, to form a screen;
The perfect backdrop for your beauty to be seen.

O speculative, tantalising, teasing sight
When life began for you with bud bound tight,
Escaping as the dawn escapes the night.

The loving cup, thy silken petals shape to form
To hold the golden nectar of the dewy morn,
That the world might drink, to celebrate when you were born.

Barney S. Smith

Death Courted

She stood before the world in all her splendour,
Breathtaking was the vision to behold;
A face expressing innocence and candour
And depth of hidden passion yet untold.

An enigmatic smile of mysticism,
An aura that bespoke of mystery deep.
A personality of vibrant magnetism,
That cloaked her, like a mantle in her sleep.

The movement of her body could turn any eye
As seductively she went upon her way.
Many silences were shattered by a heavy sigh
From both young and old men, as she passed them by.

She strode into the room where they were seated,
The innocent yet still the temptress too.
Stark passion burned quite brightly from four pairs of eyes.
Her life would end with one of them, ~ but who?

For one saw her as exciting ~ another as a whore,
Another one just saw her as his wife.
To the fourth she was a goddess, the like he had never seen before,
But fate decreed that one would end her life.

The first she teased with hidden innuendo;
To the second she became the innocent abroad;
To the third she used familiar indifference;
To the fourth she sat above him like a lord.

Death Courted cont...

And while the passions smouldered there among them
Like molten pressure on a weakened seam,
The image each had built was now among them
And for three at least, 'twould shatter every dream

As time passed, the first one rose and left them,
Both his excitement and his passion now appeased.
Soon the fourth one rose and joined him
For he could no longer stay there to be teased.

Just two left now, to woo the sultry maiden
And inside one a jealous rage did burn.
All reasoned self control was over laden,
He knew inside that he was the one that she would spurn.

An unringed hand she placed upon a nearby sleeve
And tugged at the man who saw her as his wife.
The sparkling eyes and smile said it was time to go;
They signalled too, the ending of her life.

With upward thrust, the flashing blade was driven home;
Her body fell with not a murmur or a sigh.
Unbridled savagery had spelled her doom
But could not hide the lovelight in her eye.

He'd seen her as a whore - that's what he'd told himself
Deceit to hide a needing, raging, pain
A feeling of not being good enough to give himself
Lead to the reason for his love and living, being slain.

Do Ghosts Make Love?

Where now are the spirits departed?
Are they floating on high in the air?
Are they happy or still broken hearted?
Free spirits ~ or do they still care?

Have their anguish and torments now left them?
Are they no longer bowed with dismay?
And do they make love in the heavens above,
And is it by night or by day?

What other pleasures abound them,
As they drift in ethereal bliss?
Are life's delights all around them?
Do they still get a thrill from a kiss?

And what of their moments of passion,
Are there now any there to be found?
Or are they all out of fashion,
Only left for those earthly bound?

Are there memories still there to tease them,
Of enjoyable things they have done?
Like mad passionate nights of carnal delights
Or naked romps in the sun.

Do their earthly desires all leave them?
Is their passion taken away?
Or do they still boast ,"though I'm only a ghost
I still fancy a romp in the hay."

In puzzling and asking the question,
Of whether ghosts make love;
The one place we might find the answer
Is in, WELL! HEAVENS ABOVE.

Autumn

There is a coolness in the mornings now,
And my thoughts are tinged with sadness,
At summers hastening retreat.
And the stark cold winter looming.

Quite soon the leafy bowers will disappear.
And the harvest of the hedgerows will be ending.
The early morning dews will turn to frost,
And with the cold will come the winters sleeping.

No golden corn is gleaming in the fields .
Good husbandry dictates it's gathered in.
The straw like grass has lost the lustre of it's green,
And ricks make silhouettes.
Like fortresses and castles, from an ancient scene.

The migrant birds speed swiftly by on high,
Knowing it's time for them to take their leave.
The odd reluctant one commands an almost open sky.
But soon he too must join the others in their flight,
For the larder that was his has disappeared.
And he must seek his shelter, from the dark and cheerless night.

But there is also beauty showing here.
The fading colours of the autumn glory,
Are promises of hidden peace and rest.
To gather strength that we might,
Perpetuate the never ending story.

For the autumn is the season of recall.
And there are other days and scenes, as yet to come,
As well as those enjoyed or just endured.
For my sadness is the passing of the years,
The loss, and gain, mixed up with all my hopes, and fears.

Barney S. Smith

Lost Tomorrow

I've contemplated getting old.
But always with a heavy heart.
No joy for me in ancient bones,
I'd rather from this world depart.

A tiresome burden's not my role,
At least, not as an ancient one.
For life is freedom of the soul,
And joining in creative fun.

The pleasures in this life abound,
When there is someone with which to share.
And they are blessed, are those, who've found,
Someone to love someone to share.

Alas! my dreams have passed me by.
And so I shed my silent tear.
I shut my mind to creeping age.
And crawl away to hide my fear.

Lost Control

Like the rushing torrent of a mountain stream.
The tears come forceful, spouting from the eye.
A hurricane of passions pent up force.
The dam that bursts, exploded by the feelings running high.

The intensity of raw emotions brought to view.
Exposed this once for all the world to see.
An uncontrolled demonic exhibition.
The loves, the fears, the hates inside of me.

I pray it be but once this exhibition.
This disgusting total loss of self control.
The abandonment to total erudition,
In the healing, and the cleansing, of my soul.

My solitude at least affords protection.
A slender armour for my vulnerability.
Impassioned prayer escapes my taught and trembling lips.
To guide me to the pathway of serenity.

Exhausted, and bewildered now, the tears are spent.
Tranquillity descends from heaven above.
Enveloped now in solace and content.
Wrapped in the warmth, and comfort, of your love.

Recognition

I read a book once, and the world became a different place.
I opened my eyes, and saw again the images,
That had revolved around in space.
My mind was clear, and I could see inside the real world.
No artificial splendour to hide the light of true reality.
The brilliant, blinding, searing, light of love.
Was muted soft and gentle to my sight .
By the warm and tender teardrops in my eye.
And for a while, to me, came understanding.
The harmony of love and life, were one.
Can this be then the goal that we are seeking?
The mystery of the universe revealed.
One life, One love for all.
And Love of all for one.

The Hawk And The Dove

The trees, and the sky, and the snow on the ground.
The flight of the hawk overhead.
Freedom ~ ~ ~ ~ ~ ~ But how?
Unless on the wings of a dove.
But hawks and doves cannot be one.
Unless one is inside of the other.
The airs the same, and so is flight,
And are they brave who stay to fight?
Pray God, some day, I'll see the light.
And for myself discover,
<u>ME</u>

Coloured Pictures

Surprisingly I often find,
Coloured pictures in my mind.
And more surprisingly, it seems,
I'm often dreaming coloured dreams.
For when I'm sound asleep at night,
Should not my dreams be black and white?
And lowly men cannot aspire,
To set their aims and targets higher.
For isn't it the scheme of things
That poor men only have clipped wings?
And learned cynically through bitter truth.
And chronicles of hardened youth,
That humble men are always found,
With feet placed firmly on the ground.
Oh if somehow I could be free,
To be someone else, and not be me.
I'd enter in the hall of fame
With John Livingstone Seagull as my name.
No matter that I cannot fly,
As long as spirits are soaring high.
I'd cast aside my fettered chain,
If I could live my life again.
Yet still there's hope for all mankind,
Who have coloured pictures in their mind.

Inner Universe

Hidden worlds inside my head
The world of fantasy.
Barred to all except a few,
Chosen to hold a key.
The secret world that no one knows.
Unless I allow a view,
The sheltered dreams that never show
Except to a chosen few.
And some dreams a secret never shared.
Too precious for others to see.
The inner most thoughts that can never be bared.
That are hidden from all but me.
There's the world of delight,
And the world of despairing,
The bad world of don't care,
And the good world of caring.
But the world I love best, just cannot be.
For this is a world of pure fantasy,
Where I come, and I go, with no need to hide.
For if I don't like it there, I just step outside.
And no one will know,
For many times it's been said.
"It's a good thing you don't know
What's going on in my head."
And so I survive, I go on day by day.
Just running my life, not running away.
And most times you'll find me, safely curled,
Inside my head, in my head in my favourite world..

Despair

The dark grey sky, the howling wind, the lashing rain.
Become reminders, of the deep, dark, hidden pain.
Demoralising damp, the gathering gloom.
The way uncertain as if in a darkened room.

Is there no one there to shed a light?
Must I remain alone this storm tossed night?
No one to comfort me , to hold my hand?
No one to smile and say they understand?
No one to guide or point me on my way.
Must I remain alone,? as in the day.
I'd stumbled on, and could not find the road,
Nor no one to relieve my heavy load.

Oh sleep, sweet sleep, would bring a moment of relief.
But sleep won't come to spare me from this torturous grief.
And so I stumble on 'though not too well
For I must live alone this private hell.
Although others seek to help they cannot find,
A pathway, through this twisted, tortured, mind.
And so, to the outside world I must remain,
The insane one, 'though who's to say who's sane?
Oh death, just death, can bring to me release.
To let me lie forever, in a sweet untroubled peace.

Reflections

I still cry for my lost youth.
I still despair at the creeping of age.
To die would seem the only thing, but then,
what is there in death? Is it just the cold dark
silence of putrefying flesh, or are there other
things? One way only to known: and who has
ever made the journey and travelled back again?
Would the gain repay the loss, or would there
be no gain?

Tortured flesh can bring excruciating pain, but
how does one describe the pain and torment
of a troubled mind? ~ Questions! Questions!
but no answers. And only the occasional taste
of honey on ones tongue to give succour for
other trials yet to come.
I would but sleep, but sleep its self bring only
dreams and tortures of a different kind, the half
lit world of fantasy, the macabre, that only
awakening will remove. Awake, awake to what?,
This earthly hell that mere mortals have forced
upon us? Come sweet nectar, let me press you to
my lips, that I might receive sustenance and comfort
in the short while, are true love, you take my hand
and help me conquer all.

Barney S. Smith

You've Gone

The feeling of loss now that you're not around.
The knowing I miss you so much
For the odd thing's your with me in sight and in sound.
But there's nobody near me to touch

The sound of your voice I hear on the breeze,
The catch of your breath in a sigh.
The warm sunny laughter I saw in your smile.
Like the bright summer sun in the sky.

Yes, you've gone, your not here and I miss you.
And a heavy heart's leaden with grief.
But the feeling your here is all around me,
This just adds to my great disbelief.

Your casual touch of acceptance,
Said far more than many a word.
Acknowledgement there in the gesture,
No comment, but it had said you had heard.

And time is the healer of all things.
The great equaliser of man.
And so dear friend I still miss you,
Until time brings us together again.

Absent Friends

Should there be tears? and should I weep?
For absent friends who now enjoy their deeper sleep.
Their memories come crowding back to fill my mind,
Of vagaries and penchants of another time.
Their bodies are no more, but what the hell!
Their memories come flooding back to serve me well.
No need to close my eyes to have them here,
For they are always close, so very near.
An absent face, a voice, a touch, a smile,
Come my friends, lets gather round, and stay a while.
For whilst to others it may seem you've gone
Our friendship and your influence still carries on.
And heart warming is the thought you'll always be,
A vital vibrant altruistic part of me.

Barney S. Smith

Goodbye

So this is goodbye, the nonchalant wave, the nod.
Nothing to show the internal turmoil. Oh God!
Why must we deceive, why must we hide the pain?
With the flippant aside - 'Perhaps someday I will see you again.
The pathos that's hidden in the one single word of goodbye,
The knowledge in parting that something inside you will die.
The body is heavily weighed down with internal tears,
But nature has taught us to cope with these over the years.
At least that's what we tell ourselves to help maintain the facade.
I can't be hurt says the smile, for it's put there to tell you I'm hard.
Just walking away, as if on a jaunt for the day.
While the body is screaming and begging to hear someone say,
"Goodbye is for others, it was never intended we part
Come, stay the journey, return with me now to my heart."

Friend

I've never actually said a last goodbye,
Nor heard it from someone about to die,
My final partings have been all the same;
Left with the feeling that we shall meet again.
It isn't until fate or destiny
aquaint's us with the true reality,
that thoughts of meeting loved ones face to face
must cease, and we are left an empty place;
soon, filled with heartache grief and pain
and the need to see the loved one once again.
Alas! who's there to help us in this time?
Thank God that Mother Nature dulls the mind.
Thank God for friends who offer some support,
'though their comfort at the time adds up to nought.
It isn't 'till time passes that we see
how caring, kind and generous friends can be,
and so dear friend, when you have felt rebuff
and felt that what you've offered is not enough.
take heart, for you know deep down we care
and life for is blessed because you are there.

Barney S. Smith

Dream

I gaze in awe at a young child's smile while they are at their play
lost in the dreams of a fairy tale or adventures far away.
But sadness overtakes me then, the awe turns to regret
for age has dimmed my urge to dream I often think, but yet:
there is a stirring in my heart, a great need to be free
to live my life, be what I am, to show the world just me.
The darkening gloom is lifted then and for a little while
I dream, as do the little ones, and smile to match their smile,
The magic all comes flooding back, there is music in my soul.
There is time for me to do these things, there is time to reach my goal;
a new beginning, not the end, and yes the world is fine
for there is someone now to share the dreams,
for their dream is also mine.

Lifes Clowns

Pointed hats and funny faces
dressed in filly clothes.
What is hidden underneath them
no one really knows.
Dress them smartly,
take off the make up
sit them down to find
what is there beneath the costume.
what is in their mind!
Funny jokes and silly antics,
are they there to hide
the hurt and pain of raw emotion
bottled up inside?
Glistening teardrops sparkling brightly
underneath the big top light
Is it mirth or is it sadness
hidden out of sight?
Pointed hats and painted faces,
everybody loves the clown;
life for him is one big party,
nothing ever gets him down.
Remove the hat wipe off the make-up,
look into those haunted eyes.
See the soul that's filled with sadness.
Is it such a big surprise?
Who could know his heart is aching
for the one he loved so well?
Who can know his heart is breaking?
Who's to know and who's to tell.

Barney S. Smith

Little Sad Soul

Little sad soul lost and alone;
bewildered, bemused in a world of your own.
Finding it hard to just understand
Why it is you should act like a man.
Why such a young one of sweet, tender years
Should swallow so hard to fight back the tears.
Why is it that no one can see how you feel?
That the feeling inside you is terribly real
And you are not being naughty, you are not being bad,
When all that you want is just mum and dad.
So I pray when you're older, with kids of your own,
They won't know what is' like to feel all alone.
Give them love and affection and lots of your time.
That way I know you will get along fine.
And what pride and pleasure you will feel when they say
Oh that! that's my dad and I guess he's O.K.

Lost and Alone

Lost and alone, the mind numbed by cold stark grief,
No warmth to lift the gloom, no light to show the way.
It is a dismal world that robs the right to love,
that hides the power and joy of understanding.
No change, when all around is change,
the sorrow that these words convey is etched in stone by tears,
and so, the darkness gathers overhead.
No accusation, no scorn, no blind and searing pain,
just the dark and the numbness and the tears,
but they at least bring comfort in their release,
the hot wet tears that form a pool upon the desk top.
Release! but little joy,
and so another day must end my love
too painful to endure
Thank God the strength is there to hope
no matter how low the faltering flickering shadow may appear
For there is always hope.

Barney S. Smith

Emotion

Hard to discern amongst the vibrant growth of other flesh.
Thin tissues that hide once raw mutilated wounds.
Time has done it's work to heal the gaping visual display of agony and pain.
Nothing remains, only a fading memory and the thin scarred tissues.
Weaknesses there are, hid from prying eyes,
defences to be maintained that some mortal blow may not be smitten where frailties remain.
And so it is my love with heart and soul. **Emotion**

Bluebell Wood

And I'd return there if I could
Back to those days in bluebell wood.
When you and I were seventeen
And life and the world was evergreen.

When worldly cares seemed not amiss
In the tenderness of a lover's kiss.
The caressing sun and the balmy breeze
Anonymity among the trees.

Those sweet days I still recall,
Both life and youth we had it all
And I'd return there if I could;
Back to those days in bluebell wood.

Barney S. Smith

Forgotten Dreams

Twilight thoughts of misty dreams
come floating to my mind;
other days and other ways
life of a different kind.
How oft I think of what I am
and what I used to be.
and are the things I'm doing now
really part of me?
And then I think of other things,
the things I haven't done;
like being free and being me
and living life for fun
Could I but find the courage now
to shrug and take a chance
and do the things I want to do
without a backward glance.
What then would happen to my world
and all the others there?
Would they somehow misunderstand
and think I didn't care?
It's thoughts like this that shackle me
that make me bow the knee
It's my own mind that holds me
that won't allow me to be free
to travel far, and travel wide
to horizons that are new.
To see the world with different eyes
with visions that are new,
and somehow come to life again

Forgotten Dreams cont...

breath fire in my soul.
To say just once I'm really me
at last I've reached my goal.

And yet! somewhere somehow mixed up in this
there's someone known as you,
standing on the side lines
knowing what to do.
To press the buttons pull the strings
to make it all come true.
Have courage dear just take your time
for I know that in the end
together we make it
me and my best friend.

The Family

It's good to have the family gathered round
it makes the home a much more cheerful place.
A good time, when there's lots of love around;
a special love for each familiar face.

For sad to say, these moments now are few
'though sadness isn't quite the word I'd chose.
For growing folk have many things to do
and where to spend their time is hard to chose.

No, let us say these moments now are rare.
And who dares to stop filling up with pride,
for their presence here reflects the way they care
and leaves me warm and cosy deep inside.

And there's a newer face amongst the rest
quite eager that the others will approve.
But he already know he's past the test
for there's someone here with whom he shares his love.

Soon they'll depart and go upon their way.
They'll go, but there will be something there I've found
a treasured memory for another day.
The time I had the family gathered round.

Suspended Time

Suspended time:
A journey to the past
Here and now.
How long do journeys last?
Memories evoked,
mellowed now with time,
mixed and muddled memories,
yours confused with mine.
For truth is how we see it,
to each of us our own.
The sum of life's experiences,
that is how we've grown.
Who can explain?
Who can define
'the mystic path we've trod?
Is it chance,
or pre-ordained,
or the hidden hand of God.
That lets us stumble,
picks us up,
then push us on again?
A hidden power?
a guided force?
or just the way of men
And is it written in the stars,
each one his destiny?
Or just that great commanding voice
'That what will be will be'
We climb the mountain,

Barney S. Smith

Suspended Time cont...

stroll the lane,
stand hypnotic by the shore;
and think, if fate be kind enough
there'll still be time for more.
The beginning now is history,
the future sure somehow.
And TODAY'S the time for living,
for we are in the here and now.

Pandora's Box

Why do I cry for the youth that I've lost?
Why should my eyes fill with tears
everytime that I find the thoughts in my mind,
have taken me back many years?

Nothing it seems can replace shattered dreams
nor the hope in my heart that seemed real.
Charred scars now remain where once was a flame
of burning passion and lofty ideals.

Am I mad to pursue the dreams that I knew?
To keep seeking and searching to find
the spiritual me, that longs to be free
to face life with a clear open mind.

For should I succeed, would the hunger and need
dissipate to a great empty void?
Would the pain and the tears and the anguish and fears
be the mystique, I've really enjoyed?

For how has it been, that no one's ever seen
the passion behind the wry grin?
The lust and the greed, desire, love and need
and the fear that keeps me locked in.

Is it ever to be that someone with the key
will descend from the heavens above;
and undo the locks of Pandora's box
to give me the freedom to love?

Barney S. Smith

Pandora's Box cont...

For the love within me, really has to be free
to be shared with someone of like mind.
It will be no surprise, when that one realise
that we are identically two of a kind.

So the pains and the fears, lost youth, and the tears,
stay hidden without too much fuss.
Yet there may come the day when with courage we'll say,
"Wake up world ,take a look , this is us."

Tuesday

It's Tuesday today, and we always have Tuesdays,
well, at least once a week;
And Tuesdays can only ever be that in between day.
In between like in no-mans land.
Tuesdays--------I am never sure
whether I've just come back from somewhere,
or if I should be getting excited
because soon I shall be going somewhere.
But I never know on Tuesdays.
Tuesdays are like that.
I wonder if it would have been different,
if it had been called Threesday or even Foursday,
but that might have got muddled up with Thursday.
So I suppose in a way Tuesday was right.
Although I do wish it wasn't *such* a muddle.
Perhaps I should think of changing
to some other day of the week,
That *might* help.

Muddled Mind

Migratory seasons turned upside down.
Backwards and forwards in time.
Never quite certain just where I am,
in the pattern of reason and rhyme.
Today I am here! No, 'twas yesterday.
I'm going or have I just come?
Tomorrow is here - or is it today?
And am I away or at home?
Are you here with me now, or am I alone?
My dear I really can't say
I went off this morning or did I come back?
Tell me do you expect me to stay?
Have we just said hello, or was it goodbye?
Do you wave with a tear or a smile?
And have I just told you, or is it to tell
what I have been doing the while?
Disorientation, confusion of mind
when things clear I expect I shall see.
That nothing is different, that nothing has changed.
Confusion has always been me.

Winters Tale

What does it take, I ask myself,
To make anybody aware
Of the beauty that's there for each of us?
Just how many of us care?
A different place for each of us,
the world on a winters day.
Transformed by the snow and a different light
to be viewed in another way.
Stark trees that were dark now etched in white,
as if by an artists' hand
A pen and ink drawing could best describe
this scene of a snow covered land.
Words cannot express what the eye can see;
a beauty we rarely behold.
The snow covered branches of hedges and trees
and sheep huddled close from the cold.
The unbroken snow that covers the ground
like the cloak of the vestal bride.
A white fluffy blanket that muffles all sound
yet offering no place to hide.
A landscape of beauty for all to perceive
bestowed by natures own hand.
Magical moments for us to receive.
This view of a new wonderland.

THE CHOICE IS OURS

Barney S. Smith

Springtime

The corn is greener in the fields now
and spring is moving on.
The sun is higher in the sky now
and it seems that winter's gone.
But time hangs heavy and I miss you
in spite of longer days.
The nights are empty now without you,
and I miss those old familiar ways.

Green buds are showing in the trees now
and birds parade in pairs.
Spring lambs are gambolling in the. fields now
unknown for them are earthly cares.
Still time hangs heavy and I miss you
in spite of longer days.
And nights are empty now without you,
and I miss those old familiar ways.

The golden daffodils are full now,
majestic head on slender stem.
And lovers take their evening strolls now
pert maidens with their handsome men.
So time hangs heavy and I miss you
in spite of longer days.
No wonder nights are empty now without you,
and I miss those old familiar ways.

One Man's Love

My father was born a son of the sea;
from a boy he grew to a man.
And his colour was changed to a timbered hue
by the sun, and the wind, and the sand.

He offered his life to the oceans deep.
It was there he plied his trade.
And curse he would at the howling wind,
'though he would never be afraid.

To spend his time in the company of men
To share a fishing tale
of catches that almost sank the boat,
or riding a force ten gale.

And other stories would be told
of men who are now long gone.
How they had lost their hearts and lost their lives,
to the lilt of a mermaids song.

The once horny hands are snow white now.
They are now soft where calluses grew.
With no net rope to haul, no hook to bait
and no hatches to batten too.

Tales there are of his one true love;
for tales there will always be.
As he gaze from the shore with misty eyes
At his ruling mistress - the sea.

Barney S. Smith

Remember Me

Remember me, not as I am, but how I'd like to be;
Not filled with pride nor yet filled with humility.
A man; of whom all other men might say,
"You lived your life, we would live it in no other way.
Like all the other mundane tasks in life you faced,
You met them all; and in but few were not disgraced.
You chose your path as if you knew the way,
No matter what you might encounter, day by day.
No matter either, that like all the rest
The steps you trod were not always of the best.
No matter that sometimes you tripped and fell
Undauntingly you fought your private hell
And unhesitatingly you took the test,
To solve the unsolved riddle of lifes' quest."
You pose the question, "Why should what be will be,
For we have within the right to chose our destiny?
To take up the challenge, sally forth and face the task.
To have the choice, to have the right, no need to ask
What better way to chose to end our day."
To know we have the right, the power, the voice, to say
"What you can see - well this is me - that's what I am
With no pretence, no need to fence, no need for sham"
I offer to you all just what you see.
You have the choice, you take the risk
For all that I can offer is just me.

Serenity

The mood is black as thunder and there is an air of depression.
Why must I go through these terrible mood swings.
Torn between pleasure and pain, and the sea of serenity ,
which do you chose?.
On the one hand, pleasure so intense it hurts in the most beautiful way.
Pain that is opposite, and hurts to an insufferable degree
that death would seem so easy to grasp.

On the one hand the sea of serenity, so tranquil
Where no wave or ripple **ever** make life interesting,
And on occasion, the far away feeling of loss, of being aware
that there should be something else but not knowing what;
just feeling bemused.
Then the storm clouds form overhead to tinge the sky with shadow.
But they never break or explode, just dissipate,
And never quickly enough to startle the eye with the bright gold
sunlight shimmering off a cloud.
Never quickly enough to point the way to heaven.
That rare and magical moment that can only be found
in the abandonment of one soul to another.

Oh life! why are you so cruel that having once allowed
us to taste you, we spend the rest of our lives in trying to decide
which way to go,
and perhaps dying, having never made the choice.
Could it be, that the answer lies not in this world but the next?
Is that why we are allowed an occasional glimpse of heaven,
both in passion and in serenity?

Barney S. Smith

Feasting Flight

Soft and silent as the velvet night
Marauding owls begin their feasting flight.
With hunters power in talon wing and beak
And unwinking eye to search and fix the prey they seek.

Ghost like they float, no whisper, not a sound
Just hovering a few feet from the ground.
The moving grass attracts the roving eye
and, like a stone, they plummet from the sky.

Deep down now they're buried out of sight
Lost as if swallowed by the night.
A disappearing act that makes the guess.
was this attack the one that meant success?

But no! the wraith like form is back in view
Undeterred by failure of this early coup.
The ground is raked again by searching eye
As silent wings propel him back on high.

Again and three times more, he makes the dive
But fate decrees these victims will survive.
But success for him is not far away,
for not for nothing is he named a bird of prey.
feasting flight cont.

Feasting Flight cont...

The gimlet eyes once more sweep the terrain.
Then the hurtling body's earth bound once again.
This time he's longer out of sight
dealing with his first victim of the night.

Once more the spectre rises from the ground
but this time with purpose in his flight:. He's homeward bound.
his piercing screeching cry so loud and shrill
will notify his mate he's made a kill.

The outstretched talons with relentless grip
makes certain that the precious catch won't slip.
And although he's met success he cannot rest,
for there are hungry babies in the nest.

The greedy chicks with scrawny necks outstretched
wait with wide open beaks to take the food that's fetched.
Soon nothing of this tasty morsel will remain
and parents must resume their hunting once again.

Back to resume their devastating skill
searching, seeking, anxious for another kill.
And so it continues ceaseless through the night.
For them there is no rest 'till morning light.

Barney S. Smith

Pictures In The Fire

Snapping, crackling, blazing log
Burning clear, no smoky fog.
A comfort in the cheerless night,
The dancing flame so warm and bright.

Bright coals that somehow draw my gaze
While I reminisce of bye-gone days,
And etched there in the flames I see
My life just as it used to be.

The huddled figure with grey hair
Like grandpa in his rocking chair.
The shadows on his wrinkled face,
As he sits beside the fire place.

And nanna sitting quite close by,
Nothing escaping her roving eye
As she rummages through her sewing box
For the right piece of wool to darn grandpa's socks.

The spiralling smoke changes again.
I'm no longer three, I am now about ten
But the room and the picture and the clock on the wall
Are the same as they were, they have not changed at all.

Except grandfather is looking through watery eyes
Filled with a pain he cannot disguise.
Nanna's passed on, she is no longer there
But his knarled hand still fondles the arm of her chair.
The log in the fireplace collapse in a heap
And intrudes my dreams in my wide awake sleep.
It's time now for bed, it's almost half past ten
But I know when the fire's right I'll see them again..

I Always Leave A Part Of Me Behind

I always leave a part of me behind.
I always leave a part of me behind.
Expectations often fluctuate and excitement rises high,
But I always leave a part of me behind.

Changing pictures of the scenery of places rushing by
But I always leave a part of me behind.
Despite the urgent need to travel, new experiences to find
I always leave a part of me behind.

An inner soul demanding the calm I need to find
Still I always leave a part of me behind.
Why can't I just go somewhere
And just take me away
And not have to leave a part of me behind?
But that would mean stagnation
And the closing of my mind
So I guess I must leave part of me behind.

And it seems to be the formulae of life for all mankind,
Of taking part and leaving part behind.
And our destiny was written by our forbears long ago
By them taking part and leaving part behind.

And for future generations there is in me the need to know
That I will be moving on, but leaving part behind.
And I take comfort in the knowledge that those I leave will find
Continuity from what I leave behind.

Barney S. Smith

Revealing Light

In lowly mist the hidden lands of England lie
Obscured are distant vistas from discerning eye.
Tall trees appear like spectres from another realm
But who can tell if birch or beech or oak or elm.

Gaunt houses stark and silent stand alone
A momentary glimpse is all that's shown,
As the speeding train goes rattling on its way.
No vision no nor scenery must cause delay.

The heavy vapours now begin to rise
Bringing new visions from their cloaked disguise.
A rushing brook, its icy banks display
As forcefully it hurtles on its way,

More vistas and more scenery now revealed
Of undulating land and hedge-rowed field.
Domestic beasts browse peacefully undisturbed
Each gathering strength and comfort from their common herd.

And far away a lonely figure seeks a thrill,
The mounted horseman on the distant hill.
Each glimpse that somehow helps me understand
The bounteous beauty encompassed in this sceptred land.

Medical Mystery

Long straight corridors beckoning who knows where
The smell of disinfectant and sanitised air,
Clinical cleanliness reflects in shining floor,
A name or indicator attached to every door.

Xray department, orthopaedic ward,
Obstetric clinic and others on the board.
Operating theatre, clinics for the day
Arrows and indicators pointing the way.

Another intersection, with corridors crossed
Despite the many indicators somehow I still get lost.
Two turnings left, then second right
My mind is filled with doubt.
Immense relief the finger points 'Ahead to this way out'

A few more steps then through the doors
A sigh of great relief.
The news I've heard ,almost every word,
I've heard in disbelief.

"We are pleased to say that your O.K.
The others are much worse.
You have passed the test on your first day
You are now a student nurse."

Barney S. Smith

Forever Friend

The eyes were as bright as they'd always been
Although life was ebbing away.
The welcoming smile expressed the words
That the tired voice could not say.

The warmth of the touch as lips brushed the cheek,
The gentle squeeze of the hand.
No need for either of them to speak
Each knew that they'd understand.

In those moments together the years rolled away
As if they had never been.
He was once more again a man in his prime
And she just a girl in her teens.

The love shared between them but never expressed
It was a love that they knew would not end.
Not the love of a lover, or mistress, or wife,
But the love of a very dear friend.

This final reminder of the pleasure they'd shared
In each others company.
The uninvolved way that each of them cared,
Was there for all to see.

Their moments together were happy and good
Something death itself could not end;
And the unspoken promise that each understood
That they will be always together as friends.

You Are

There is nothing will convey,
The words I want to say
Nothing more than just
'YOU ARE'

You hold my destiny
For the creative part of me.
My internal melody says
'YOU ARE'

I've searched the oceans far and wide
Restless as the surging tide;
Just to hold you here inside
For YOU ARE part of me.

You are the very air I breathe,
You are all that I believe.
All I see all I perceive;
You are the heart of me.

As I live and breathe and die
No matter how I try.
Only two words say it all
'YOU ARE'!

Barney S. Smith

Tomorrow Is Our Goodbye

The flame from the candle light flickers
Reflecting the tear in your eye,
For it is almost tomorrow
And tomorrow is our goodbye.

To hold you again for the last time;
To feel your soft hair on my cheek
And unspoken words stay unspoken,
For neither is willing to speak.

And it's magic that holds us together
The power of sheer fantasy
Could it only be this way forever
But we know that it isn't to be

For the first time I find love, I lose love;
Just like building then tearing apart.
But there's one part that's safely inside me
You will always be here in my heart.

Choices

Are the choices we make in life
sometimes made when all hope is gone?
When there are no more reserves.
When it's futile to just carry on.
When you've given your best
but your best is just not good enough.
When all fight has gone
'cause the going is really too tough.
When you look for a friend
but there is no friend to be found.
When you are seeking for help
but the help that you seek's not around.
When decision is yours
but decision is really too hard.
That the choices you make
must be made without any regard
to the way that you feel,
or the best way to meet your own need.
For if you chose for yourself
then your motive is tainted with greed.
For the choice that is made
is always for some other one,
and a choice for one's self
is something that just is not done.
And in giving to others
with no due regard for the cost,
No choice for one's love
must end in a loved one being lost.

Quaker Wedding

No beating drum,
No triumphal wedding march,
No parade through sabre forming arch.
A greater victory for love and peace.
A vow midst friends
To help ensure that inner conflicts cease.
A sharing
Of the embryonic new pledged structured life,
With simple words
Your status changed to man and wife.
And strength was there
Though not portrayed as might.
A quiet strength
That seemed to say somehow,
That both the silence and the words were right.
And each one there
Allowed to hold or share their thought
Of your special day.
And of the warmth and love you'd brought
And this reflected back from all those there;
This very special love for all to share.
The joy and pleasure there for all
The chance to say,
That friends made friends with **'Friends'**
Upon your wedding day.

The New House

The new house has a new mistress
Though it's not very often she's seen.
For the curtains are drawn when I visit
And the doors are enclosed by a screen.
I tried to engage conversation
But the lady was not to be drawn.
She says she has no inclination
As she covered her mouth in a yawn.
I begged her pray let me enter
But she, her pretty head shook.
'I could be no more contented
Here alone by myself with a book'
I again begged please let me enter.
She tossed back her head and she laughed,
'You are only a great tormentor
And to open the door would be daft'.
For a full day or so I pleaded
Like a man who pleads for his life.
Then the unyielding door was opened
And I entered and embraced my wife.

Victims

Predators menacingly prowling;
Flee victim flee.
Hear their calls spine chilling howling;
Flee victims flee.

Haunting spectres of the night;
See victims see.
Danger lurking out of sight;
See victims see.

Transfixed by hypnotic eye;
Run victim run.
Don't delay, you stay, you die;
Run victim run.

Ripping talon beak or blade;
Die victim die.
In alleyway or leafy glade;
Die victim die.

Fear had made of you a slave;
'Bye victim 'bye.
Fear that takes you to your grave;
'Bye victim 'bye.

What Of The Maid

The Rams are a tupping,
The stags are a rutting,
The mating season's begun.
And all the young braves
Are holding their raves
And thinking that life is such fun,

But what of the maid,
The one being laid?
And what of the ewe and the doe?
Do they enjoy
The same as the boy
Or do they prefer to say no?

And would it transpire
That a male filled with desire,
Stop to listen to the maids plea?
Or would he just do
What he wanted too
Saying it's not for you, it's for me?

Or was it natures plan
Just to satisfy man?
Did she think of the female as well?
Or is it simply the truth
That love is for both?
If it were not then life would be hell!

Barney S. Smith

Life

I stopped living for a while
But never stopped loving.
I have a tree in my garden
Perhaps not a tree - more of a sapling.
Watching it grow reminds me of where I am,
Not growing all the while, but occasionally resting.

I met a friend the other day
He said, "You're looking older."
Honesty is what I need from friends.
I really am no longer in the springtime of my youth
For 'though truth may hurt, it very rare offends.

And it's nice to let my mind run wild,
To let it go where ever.
Not to have it cluttered up with things;
But just to travel with myself,
Body, mind and spirit.
To be not too concerned with what each new day brings.

I've lived my life a hundred times
And other peoples too.
Each time I find mine's betterer than theirs.
I haven't got their wealth and things
Nor their good looks and brains,
But most of all I haven't got their cares.

My thoughts are mine, my world is mine,
It isn't someone else's.
And isn't that the way that things should be?
And when the world calls out with glee,
"I know who you are."
They can only know the bits I let them see.

Take My Hand

Take my hand for once time's sake.
Come to me and let us love.
These precious moments let us take
To savour in the taste of love.

Sweet moments still in ageless time.
That innocence in love sublime.
Delights of life for us to share:
We took them all we had them there.

But time! the challenger of man
Holds up his hand with mocking smile.
Enjoy forever if you can
But pleasure only lasts awhile.

We fight with time, we give him hell,
And yes - we manage very well.
Though on occasion we may lose
Pleasures return when pleasures chose.

A touch a smile from you or I
Will trigger off that sweet recall.
And illuminate the memory
Of the time we had it all.

So let us stay the closing door
And hold back time - we have before.
Let us enjoy the ecstasy
That's held in our twinning destiny.

So take my hand for once time's sak.e
Come to me and let us love.
These precious moments let us take
To savour in the taste of love.

Barney S. Smith

Spring Has Begun

Spring is this morning.
The light and the sun
And smiles on the faces
Says spring has begun.

The birds in the hedgerows
Not flocking - but pairs,
While magpies are mocking
All worldly cares.

The green is much greener
In field and on tree,
And flowers are blooming
As bright as can be.

The larks are a - singing
And soaring above.
And unrehearsed people
Are falling in love.

For some it's a new love,
For others it's old.
And all sorts are smitten
Both timid and bold.

Lambs are a - gambolling,
Frisking in play.
Filled with exuberance
At the joy of the day.

For spring is this morning,
The light and the sun
And the smiles on the faces
Says spring has begun.

Swallows on the wire

Swallows on the wire,
Swifts in the air.
Summer is a - hastening.
Blossom scent is in the ai.r

The sun is in the heavens.
The earth is bathed in light.
A gentle warmth pervades me
I know that all is right.

Multi coloured hedgerows
Shimmering in the sun.
Full blossom and a - changing leaf
Suggest spring is almost done.

Busy, buzzing insects
Beetles, bees and flies,
Appear as if from nowhere
Before your very eyes.

Domestic beasts a-browsing
Warmed by the morning sun.
A scene of real contentment
There for everyone.

A solitary farmer
Working in his field,
Tending well his seedlings
To ensure a greater yield.

Sun and light and springtime,
Summer on the way.
A treasure to remember
This almost perfect day.

Barney S. Smith

Christmas

Emotions at Christmas,
Looks of surprise,
Smiles on the faces,
Tears in the eyes.

Dreams of the hopeful,
The wistful 'If only',
Joy for fulfilled ones.
Fears for the lonely.

Hearts filled with loving,
Heads filled with thought.
The joys and the sadness
That Christmas has brought.

Some families together
And others excited,
That just for a while
They might be united.

And Christmas the time
Of giving and sharing.
The time to be 'there'
And to carry on caring.

Countryside

The countryside is beautiful now in summertime,
The colours are so iridescent bright.
The golden shimmering corn is of an ageless time
That bathes the world in gold reflected light.

The dark green leaves on trees tells us that spring has gone.
High Summer's now, when everything appears full grown.
The meadows clothed in buttercups have taken on
A fullness and a colour of their own.

And people too resplendent in their summer wear
They compliment the colours of the summer flowers.
And nature in her wisdom, and to show she cares
Displays the beauties in extended daylight hours.

Barney S. Smith

And Will There Be A Heaven There For Me

And soon I too shall die and be no more,
My scant remains entombed beneath the sod.
And will there be a heaven there for me?
And shall I see the smiling face of God?

Rhetorical I feel the questions posed.
No answer for a non believer such as I.
'Tis said that only ever one came back
For mere mortals, there is only one goodbye.

No sadness though whilst musing on my fate.
For I am the sum total of my past,
And somewhere further in my progeny
I am sure a little bit of me will last.

For it has been a good life all in all.
I feel quite pleased to say that I was here.
And maybe there are better things to come
'Though those that're passed have left me with good cheer.

Take heart dear friends, I've no intention yet
As Shakespeare said 'To quit this mortal coil'.
Fulfilment of my life is still my aim
And I shall stay until I reach my goal.

Unfinished business still for me to do
I owe it all to those I hold so dear,
So I'll not end by saying, "see you soon"
But by saying,"See you all again next year."
With Love And Best Wishes

Summer -94

Summer 94 and---------------
Heat.
Memories so bitter--------------
Sweet.
Another year of life is--------------
Gone.
The future with its finger beckons--------------
On.
Ambitions dreams and hopes are--------------
Still
Alive within us too/two/to--------------
Fulfil.
And of future dreams or are they--------------
Past?
Are they to be fulfilled--------------
At last?
Or have they passed beyond--------------
Recall?
Or do you still remember--------------
all
The melodies we played--------------
In tune.
Can we replay them once more--------------
Soon?
There is no need for me to ask--------------
I guess,
For you and I know that the answer will be--------------
Yes.

Barney S. Smith

To London

Today I travelled on the train to London.
Allowing me to see the English countryside again
The morning cool, and bright, and hints of autumn.
Cloud patterns hint of far approaching rain.

The subtle changing colours of the landscape.
Old stubble now has moved from gold to brown and green.
Migrating geese have gathered for a fuelling feast
And very soon they'll leave this pastoral scene.

The speeding train passes by a field of lavender,
The purple bloom brings colour-adds to autumn hues.
The still remaining swallow swiftly flashes by
Like a speeding messenger with important news.

Rural England! Is there anywhere in this world a better place
To raise the ghosts and spectres of the past?
The aspirations hopes and dreams of bye gone days
Are set in scenes that reassures that some things last.

80

Tapestry

Scribbling words describing life;
Teasing torments, struggles, strife,
Sadness, madness, guilt and pain
Memory brings them back again.
Leisure, pleasure, love and joy;
Boisterous, noisy, shy and coy.
Many persons, or only one,
Who suffers pain yet enjoys fun.
Teasing, pleasing, becomes an art.
A tapestry of which life's a part.
Black and white and love and hate,
Becomes a part of each ones fate.
Travelling both far and wide
In reality, or just inside.
Each one brave and each afraid
Heredity or just self-made.
Each one asks both where and why.
But the biggest question, "Who am I?"
Remains unanswered for a while.
Then we discover with a smile
That, what in life will be, will be.
To be myself **I must know me.**

Barney S. Smith

Mark Time

Fall in all those who have marked time with their lives,
Or those who feel they have to mark time now.
Stand up all those who have no where to go
And those who have but can't because they don't know how.
Look deep inside and ask yourself the question,
"What do I need to push me on my way?"
Who spreads the fear that seem to keep me stranded
That makes me say perhaps another day?
Believe it's true that life is one time only;
If I lose a day it cannot be replaced.
And dreaded fear, remains a fear forever
With out the strength to meet it face to face.
So, step forward now with head upheld and ready.
It doesn't matter if your panic shows.
Just stand your ground, don't falter, remain steady
With faith and self belief, your fear will go.

Questions and Answers

Question and answer,
Lifes little game:
All those I meet
Are just the same.

Will you or won't you?
You will if you can.
This age old custom
Still played by man.

Do you or don't you?
That's how the game goes.
You have or You haven't
Everyone knows.

It's a way of connecting,
We are all the same
Whatever the question,
We are playing the game.

It's the same with the answers
That everyone knows,
I will if you will:
All right; I suppose.

I did or I didn't
At sometime we'll say,
Still playing the game
In the time honoured way,

We all need acceptance
For we are all the same,
And we all know we'll find it
Just playing the game.

Barney S. Smith

Is it Good or Bad to Be Me

You are fat and you're old and you're ugly
I tell myself every day.
You are fat and you're old and you're ugly
And what hair you have left's turned to grey.

You are fat and you're old and you're ugly
It is there for all to see.
You are fat and you're old and you're ugly
Who would want to be me?

You are cuddly and wise and you're handsome
At least that's what my friends say.
You are cuddly and wise and you're handsome
A message I get day by day.

You are cuddly and wise and you're handsome
And also you're really quite tall.
You are cuddly and wise and you're handsome
And it's not bad to be me at all!

Lost And Found

Where are you now
The friend that I have lost?
This startling memory
From the dim and distant past.

When did we last meet
And has it been so long?
Yet still I can see you
In the words of every song.

Why am I reminded
By a poem or a tree,
That somewhere deep inside me
You are very much a part of me?

And time is like a shadow
Sometimes short and sometimes long.
Short when I am with you.
Long now you have gone.

Did we share those times together
Or are they just a dream?
Clear or muddied fantasy
Like the waters in a stream.

How can I contain you.
You spectre from the past?
When you return to haunt me
To show me what I've lost?

Barney S. Smith

Lost and Found cont...

But then there are other times I've found you,
Times when I have smiled
When we have found our freedom
My trapped and restless inner child.

I know my friend you are still around
You are not too far away;
And someday I will find you
Oh! happy, happy day.

For I'll be you and you'll be me,
Together we will be one,
And share our days in happy ways
Together - - having fun.

And the world will be a happy place.
And there will be no end
When we are back together,
Me and my long lost new found friend.

Lost Love

Time is no more for a love that's gone
That slipped away into the past;
It's for those that are left to weep and mourn
To deny the dream that could not last.

For time befriends the adventurous ones
The bold ones with the gleaming eye.
Their unfurled banners proclaim their love,
For them there is no time to die.

The richness of life is in their blood.
No task too great to overcome.
For them the taste of life is good,
Their strength demands their will be done.

So be brave, be true and follow your star
Discover the spirit within.
The hardest battle is the one with ones self.
It's the one we all have to win.

Barney S. Smith

1948 Numero Uno

I was really sad and lonely
'til the first day I met you.
It was thinking of you only
That kept me smiling through.
I did not think you cared for me
That Sunday afternoon,
But many things have happened since
To change my mind so soon.
The bridge we laid, the plans we made.
Where next again we'd meet.
A country walk, a lovers talk
And all our friends we'd meet.

Still Crazy

Jazz come cool and you can mock
But without that swing we don't get rock.
Without that stuff back in the can
There'd be no heavy metal man.

Still crazy; still crazy, crazy mean.
I'm back but I don't know where I've been,
What I've done, or who I've seen. Still crazy.

I know my music history's hazy,
But nothings changed, we're all still crazy.
For crazy is as crazy does
But the whole damn thing still gives a buzz.

Still crazy; still crazy, crazy mean.
I'm back but I don't know where I've been.
What I've done, or who I've seen.
Still crazy.

Just let go and think back when you were only nine or ten.
What kind of things gave you a fix what drove you wild and gave you kicks.
When oldies gave you kinda hell, you'd just lay back 'n scream 'n yell.
Still crazy.

And when you moved into your teens
And holy man what did that mean?
You'd try the fizz and eye the chicks
And scam the most amazing tricks.

Barney S. Smith

Still Crazy cont...

Still crazy; still crazy, crazy mean.
I'm back but I don't know where I've been.
What I've done, or who I've seen.
Still crazy.

Now when you think your past the crown, you'll throttle back and settle down.
Some bum comes thrashin up a sound, plays hell and kicks the fences down.
It's time to quit the hanging around, you just gear up and do the town.
Still crazy.

Flat down - you got no energy.
You think this trip is not for me
And then you shake the foggy muzz
The whole damn thing still gives a buzz.

Still crazy, still crazy, crazy mean.
I'm back but I don't know where I've been,
What I've done, or who I've seen.
Still crazy.

Your knowing that you can't let go.
Your knowing what you got ta do.
You knowing you 'aint got a chance
Unless you just let go and join the dance.

Still crazy, still crazy, crazy mean.
I'm back - but I don't know where I've been,
What I've done, or who I've seen.
Still crazy.

Still Crazy cont...

Still crazy, still crazy, crazy mean.
I'm back - but don't know where I've been.
What I've done, or who I've seen.
Still crazy.

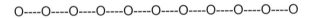

alternative chorus
Still crazy, their crazy, mad crazy.
They say that when I'm down or high or ill,
That all I do is pop a pill, or grab a can and take a swill.
They're crazy.

my musical advisor advises me that lyrics follow a pattern of :-

verse chorus verse chorus M/8 verse chorus M/8 verse chorus chorus

M/8 = eight to the bar

Just Like Coming Home

Strange things keep coming back to me.
They come alive now in my memory,
The things I thought I'd never see.
It's just like coming home.

I'm coming home and never going away,
And when I'm there that's where I'm going to stay.
The wisest words you'll ever hear me say,
"I'm safely home at last".

Like a journey in space as you ride on a star
You are standing still, but you are travelling far
All is new - but familiar you know where you are.
It's just like coming home.

I'm coming home and never going away,
And when I'm there that's where I'm going to stay.
The wisest words you'll ever hear me say,
"I'm safely home at last".

As you speed around the universe, from one world to the next,
A calmness pervades you, you are never perplexed.
A whole life in one journey, the whole thing projected.
You're calm and you're safe, the whole thing is protected.
The battle is finished, the raging is done,
The internal peace proclaims you have won.

The star wars are over, the galaxy saved.
There's freedom for everyone, no one is enslaved.
A euphoric feeling of peace now pervades.
It's just like coming home.

Just like coming home cont...

I'm coming home and never going away,
And when I'm there that's where I'm going to stay.
The wisest words you'll ever hear me say,
"I'm safely home at last".

All internal battles can now at last cease.
The conflict is over, I've found internal peace.
The shackles are gone, cast off and thrown,
With a crowd or just me, I am never alone.
The battle is over, the raging is done,
The internal peace proclaims I have won.

There is Venus and Pluto, Mercury and Mars
And all is at peace with the planets and stars.
There are no more prisons or handcuffs or bars.
It's just like coming home.

I'm coming home and never going away,
And when I'm there that's where I'm going to stay.
The wisest words you'll ever hear me say.
"I'm safely home at last"

New Love

I knew I just had to have her
For me it was love at first sight.
She became my first thought every morning
And kept me awake every night.

Her body was fashioned in heaven,
Her profile just blew my mind.
From the front she was really quite gorgeous.
Who could ever describe her behind?

When I touched her she was so responsive
Just silent with no word to say.
The first time I entered inside her
It fair blew my whole mind away.

I called at the place she resided.
With a smile, "And have a nice day".
I adjusted the seat and the mirror
And drove my new loved one away.

When Infatuation Turns To Love

Where were we when I saw the glance
That told me that I had a chance
To follow through this odd sensation
That would lead us to infatuation

You were well aware and so was I
We could not let this chance slip by
We responded to the situation
And surrendered to infatuation

The world became a different place
For every where I saw your face
In clouds and streams and imagination
Could this really be infatuation

Then love came like a total stranger
What fools! we did not see the danger
Bewilderment and consternation
What happened to infatuation

A different game so hard to play
The pain of pleasure every day
There was no hint no expectation
That love would lead us from infatuation

'though love has won we both are losers
For love dictates we must be chosers
To chose love we live in condemnation
No safety now in infatuation

Barney S. Smith

The Game Of Love

I' never tasted love
I'd only wasted love
I wanted to haste to love
Oh! could it be

Here in the game of love
We shared the name of love
Both madly insane with love
It's ecstasy

What do we know of love
The highs and lows of love
How can I show her love
My destiny

We are confused by love
Lost and bemused by love
Hurt and abused by love
Both you and me

What do we gain of love
Nought but the pain of love
All that remains of love
Is misery

Like storms we're tossed by love
When we have lost to love
Who counts the cost of love
Oh pity me

When Infatuation Plays The Game Of Love

Where were we when I saw the glance
That told me that I had a chance
To follow through this odd sensation
That would lead us to infatuation

I'd never tasted love
I'd only wasted love
I wanted to haste to love
Oh! could it be

You were well aware and so was I
We could not let this chance slip by
We responded to the situation
And surrendered to infatuation

Here in the game of love
We shared the name of love
Both madly insane with love
It's ecstasy

The world became a different place
For every where I saw your face
In clouds and streams and imagination
Could this really be infatuation

What do we know of love
The highs and lows of love
How can I show her love
My destiny

Barney S. Smith

When Infatuation Plays The Game Of Love cont...

Then love came like a total stranger
What fools! we did not see the danger
Bewilderment and consternation
What happened to infatuation

We are confused by love
Lost and bemused by love
Hurt and abused by love
Both you and me

A different game so hard to play
The pain of pleasure every day
There was no hint no expectation
That love would lead us from infatuation

What do we gain of love
Nought but the pain of love
All that remains of love
Is misery

'though love has won we both are losers
For love dictates we must be chosers
TO chose love we live in condemnation
No safety now in infatuation

Like storms we're tossed by love
When we have lost to love
Who counts the cost of love
Oh pity me.

Juxtaposition

Whence comes this insane tragedy
That separates myself from me?
Too early made ~ the interpretation,
To allow myself the integration.

My inner world and hidden self,
Some forgotten parcel on a hidden shelf.
Wrapped in fear so no one should see
The pain and hurt of my misery.

For who could bear their looks of sadness?
If they should glimpse my internal madness.
The shame, the guilt, so terrifying,
The acts of bravado, the constant denying.

This interminable battle to be free,
To guard myself from their sympathy.
One tiny attempt at humiliation
Would lead only to my annihilation.

I fight the battle I know the plan,
The inner struggle of all man.
In searching for their own salvation,
By finding release in integration.

What of the other world out there?
The communal one we all must share.
For without you there is no me,
So I must display for all to see

Barney S. Smith

Juxtaposition cont...

How do I know how to get it right
Do I acquiesce or stand and fight?
Yes sir no sir three bags full
When I see a bird *Do I have* to pull?

Must I enjoin in lifes silly game,
Just to burden myself with my internal shame?
To open my arms and plead to be kissed
Just to prove to myself I really exist.

Be quite outrageous to make people stare,
Just to prove to myself I really am there.
To stand up and challenge when all I want is to run
Being seen as a hard bastard is really not fun.

Why can't I accept that I am safe and sound
That I am not really lost and need to be found?
I just need to fall asleep every night
Knowing I'm me and *Me* is all right.

To Answer The Call

Oceans that race 'neath a wind that sigh.
White fluffy clouds in a clear blue sky,
And fellow adventurers go sailing by
But I'm all alone in my world am I.

Wild galloping horses riding the sea,
Tossing their white mains for all to see.
Where next am I going where will it be
I need the excitement rising in me.

Some tropical island some far away shore,
Some strange far distant land I've not seen before
Or will I end up in my home port once more
To find that dry land is a bit of a bore?

To play once again the tense waiting game.
Attentively listening should I hear my name,
To answer the call to go and seek fame.
Knowing if it doesn't succeed then there's no one to blame.

The dream of the dreamer is there in us all.
Nurtured and cherished from when we were small.
With the dream in our eye we want to walk tall,
And we know we are ready to answer the call.

When life's true journey has really begun
When heart stopping adventure is part of the fun
When there's no time to measure the things that you've done
Just follow your spirit and let the thing run

Be alert to all things whether big ones or small
Be aware of your senses be aware of them all
Hark back to your memories for total recall
And you will be ready to answer the call

Barney S. Smith

Loves Mistake

A stormy night, the candle light
And two to dine.
A moon to rise, two shining eyes
A sparking wine.
A world away, where we could stay
A love sublime

For here at last, the stormy past
Had reached it's calms.
The music played, our bodies swayed,
Beneath the palms
The whispered words that we had shared
Raised no alarms.

The seductive smile, could still beguile
The smile said yes.
How could I know, she might say no
I couldn't guess.
The urge so strong, I'd got it wrong
I must confess.

'You've got it wrong, the pain's too strong
I can't forget.
It's far too late, I just feel hate
That's all you'll get.
Why can't you see , I just wish we
Had never met'.

Loves mistake cont...

'All I can say, is go away
All love is gone.
There's someone new, he's far more true
He's the only one.
I paid the cost' so just get lost
I'm having fun.

I'm on my own, she must have known
I did her wrong.
She'd been bereft, that I had left
Her far too long.
I'd no idea, her hate and fear
Could be so strong.

Should I replace that haunting face
With someone new.
My aching heart, says from the start
What I must do.
Learn from the past, to stand steadfast
And be always true.

A Fool and A Mole

I will tell you a secret,
You will think I'm a fool.
I fell in love with a little black mole.

The first time I saw her
I yelled with delight.
For I had never seen
Such an entrancing sight.

On the right bank of the river
She made her home,
And 'though often invited
She never would roam.

So we would spend time together
With hardly a word.
For to speak with a mole
Seemed rather absurd.

So I would just sit and stroke her
I loved her so much,
And I found such delight
In her soft velvety touch.

She would just sit and take it
With never a sigh.
And remain quite unperturbed
As the traffic passed by.

A Fool and A Mole cont...

Now sadly she's left me
And I'm all alone
But I picture her there
In her little dark home

I just keep hoping and dreaming
That one day she might,
Allow me once more
That wonderful sight.

That she might pick up courage
And come out of her hole.
So I could be re-united
With my little black mole.

Barney S. Smith

Crazy About You

What's insane? What's sanity?
The way we are or used to be?
For nothings clear except you and me.
Still crazy about you.

I drift around now on my own.
But it's not good to be alone,
To feel my heart like heavy stone.
Still crazy about you.

What happened that we can't touch base?
Was I such a sad and sorry case?
I'm crying now _ I see your face.
Still crazy about you.

I look around your standing there,
I stretch my arm to touch your hair.
You shrug your shoulders you don't care.
Still crazy about you.

No sanity, I'm just insane.
Trapped now in the crying game,
So I'm the only one to blame.
Still crazy about you.

Tupping Time

"Why do they make me wear this bag?"
It wobbles like a jelly.
They've gone and filled it up with dye,
And strapped it to my belly.

It's tupping time, it's tupping time,
For us gay rams life is sublime.
I may miss one but I'll get nine,
I love my tup at tupping time.

The farmer feeds me his best hay
And tells me I must earn my pay.
I must keep at it night and day.
I gotta keep on tupping.

It's tupping, time it's tupping time,
For us gay rams life is sublime.
I may miss one but I'll get nine.
I love my tup at tupping time.

The ewes lead me a merry dance,
Look down their nose at me askance.
But I catch their eye and take my chance,
For I know they all want tupping.

It's tupping time, it's tupping time,
For us gay rams life is sublime.
I may miss one but I'll get nine.
I love my tup at tupping time.

Barney S. Smith

Tupping Time cont...

Some try to keep their modesty
By remaining pure and clean.
But the dye will blot their copy book
And show me where I've been.

It's tupping time, it's tupping time,
For us gay rams life is sublime.
I may miss one but I'll get nine.
I love my tup at tupping time.

The white backs now are disappearing fast,
The farmer counts as they go past.
If I dump my dye I can make it last,
And I can go on tupping.

It's tupping time, it's tupping time,
For us gay rams life is sublime.
I may miss one but I'll get nine.
I love my tup at tupping time.

Road Of Life

A shadow passes on the road to happiness,
A dark cloud's cast upon the path of love.
But we, with love, and patience, faith and tenderness
Can conquer all the shadows from above.

For we have strolled along the paths of beauty,
Enchanted as we wandered in the dell.
But alas! we lost the way our path of duty
And dimmed the vision of the magic spell.

But time, our love and faith shall strengthen,
And darkness and despair shall fade and wane.
And our moments of happiness shall lengthen,
When we are on the straight and true road once again.

Buttercups

I shall never gaze upon the flower of the buttercup again,
Least sweet memories and thoughts light up my eye.
For the golden shimmering petals will remind me when
The hands of time stood still, for you and I.

The leafy path, just off the road, wound up the hill.
Your hand in mine you helped me on the way.
We climbed the bowered stairway to our wonderland
To create a treasured memory of that day.

We left the path and found a place to view the scene,
An idyll spot put there for you and me.
And we laid together in the sea of gold and green
And floated gently to our world of fantasy.

The flowered hedgerows filled with melodies of singing birds;
Their songs were only meant for you and I to hear.
And with the clear blue sky a blanket overhead
Perfection of the day was very near.

We gazed into each others eyes with mute consent.
And passion played upon the summit of that hill.
Contentment came to both of us with passion spent.
That **magic** day, mid buttercups, when time stood still.

How Can I Tell You I Love You?

How can I tell you I love you
In a way that you understand?
Or share the thrill of the feeling
That I get from the touch of your hand.

The blissful content that invades me
When I am lost in the depth of your eye.
Or the magical journey you take me
When I am caught on the breath of your sigh.

Great warm loving feelings enfold me
At the merest sound of your voice;
And the chuckling notes of your laughter
Invites the world to rejoice.

The strength that your presence engenders.
The power of your total support.
The pleasure of just being with you,
Is a treasure that cannot be bought.

So there is warmth and comfort inside me,
Just knowing you're close at hand.
How can I tell you I love you ,
In a way that you'll understand?

Barney S. Smith

For Michael

I've tried so hard to know my feelings.
I have looked for reasons to explain.
Although I have searched, I have found no meaning.
The pain of not knowing still remain.

I never saw your smile, or held your hand.
We had no time to understand.
For a fleeting moment you were there,
And that one moment we could not share.

If only I had had the chance
To hold you close, or share a glance.
Of knowing.
Understanding what things meant.
Why you were there but so quickly went.

Oh! so quickly you had to go.
Without even the chance to say 'Hello'.
And forever I will never know
Just why it was you had to go.

What colour hair? what colour eyes?
In innocence with no disguise.
So small, but with so much potential.
Divine intent or intervention?

And years go bye, time quickly flies,
But never a chance for our goodbyes.
And you've been there with me through the years.
In a heart filled with love and silent tears.

A Special Birthday

So now you are seventy,
And I'm seventy too,(or should that be two)
Your hair may be white
But your eyes are still blue.

The smile on your lips
Has managed to stay,
And the smile in your eyes
Still lights up each day.

Tasks may take longer,
But no one would know.
And the body's less supple
But it doesn't show.

The mind's still alert,
And the wit is still there.
When there are things to be done,
You do more than your share.

The garden, the housework,
The things from the shop.
And it's just 'cause I nag
That I get you to stop.

So I say 'When I was your age,
I did that too.
But I can't do it now,
Because I am older than you.

Significantly

Twenty fifth of November, two thousand and three.
The day had begun insignificantly.
A usual day with a usual routine,
That's how it was, how the morning had been.

No hint of the trauma ~ the forceful impact,
How a programme on TV would make me re-act.
A programme of pleasure ~ a place in the sun,
Somewhere to escape too ~ to take time out for fun.

How could I know that the idyllic scenes,
Would be able to shatter a life time of dreams.
Dreams that were nurtured with each working day.
That at the end of my time I'd find somewhere to play.

I know now with time how the image had grown.
But you must share a dream it's no good on your own.
Unspoken dreams I thought both of us knew.
That your partner would want the same things to do.

So you work hard together, you plan and you scheme.
Not thinking that each had a separate dream.
A place in the garden, or a place in the sun.
You can't have them both, you can only have one.

It's like sharing a journey, or sharing a task.
You both think it's the same, but you don't bother to ask.
It's time for decisions, to go, or to stay?
Which means somebody's dream, will be blown away.

Negotiations are over, the talking is done.
I've said goodbye to my place in the sun.
Fate has decided that what will be, will be,
And a lesson is learned quite significantly.

Autumn's Child

Blackberrying, or brambling,
As a friend prefers to say.
Is time to enjoy nature
In a different kind of way.

The gathering of wild fruits
Give a sense of satisfaction.
A simple pastime, still enjoyed.
With the minimum of action.

A time to spend time with myself
In quiet reminiscing.
A pleasure that I'd thought I'd lost
For lately it's been missing.

Hedgerow and field spell out for me
The message of natures rhyme.
For spring and summer are well gone
On the passages of time.

Gold stubble where the corn once grew,
Laid bare for winter's resting.
And hedgerows with daily changing hue
No longer used for nesting.

Yet still there is a harvest here,
Of blackberry and sloe,
Where hip and haw and damson,
And wild elderberries grow.

My basket is quite full now,
I realise with a sigh.
My time for me, is over,
So it's home for blackberry and apple pie.

Barney S. Smith

Cliff Top

Stationed there along the cliff top
Seats for aged folk to rest.
Assorted hats to ward off sunstroke,
Chins resting snugly on their chests.

Time for them to sit there pondering,
Silently beside the shore.
Remembering and quietly wondering
Of the many things that went before.

Images of past acquaintance
Fly unbidden to the mind.
Far more gone than those still with us.
Not many now are left behind.

Seated here above the shore line
Memory plays a trick or two.
Imagination still allows us
To do the things we used to do.

To swim out to the marker buoys,
Play footie on the sand,
To scoop up shrimps from rocky pools.
Feel them squiggle in your hands.

See jelly-fish go floating by
Transparent in the sun.
"Look out, they'll sting" goes the cry,
But it's shouted out in fun.

Cliff top cont...

The starfish washed up by the tide,
Bright orange through to white,
Lie patiently along the shore
For their return to the sky at night.

There are shells to gather by the score.
Mussels, whelk and winkle,
Crab, limpet, razor and many more,
All along the shore they're sprinkled.

Then it's hard to believe your eye
As a school of porpoises swim by.
On that glad note we must away.
A near perfect end to a perfect day.

All that's needed now, you tell yourself,
To make the day complete.
Is to hurry home and tell your mate
But you are stuck fast on the seat.

Barney S. Smith

Redemption

I cried myself to sleep last night
The first time for a while.
It came as such a great relief
Not to hide behind a smile.

The cleansing tears were needed
For I'd read the word redemption,
And the inner voice was saying
For me there's no exemption.

There is no place that's big enough
To run away and hide.
Believe me, I'm an expert,
Far too many times I've tried.

Redemption! how it haunts me.
I can not maintain postponement,
For time is running out on me
As I search for my atonement.

How difficult to right a wrong.
For where does one begin
When there from the beginning
Life was filled with sin?

I just can't do it, it's too hard.
Too hard to even try.
Why be a fool and tell the truth
When it's easier to lie.

Redemption cont...

But terror of discovery
Of the wrongs that I have done.
They'll be declared to all the world
I'll be shunned by everyone.

I see the flames of hell rise up
And Satan beckons me.
I must find my redemption
Or I'll end in purgatory.

So back to tears for solace
And continuation of the fight.
For I must try, before I die,
To get the whole thing right.

Barney S. Smith

Fair and Lovely

Now that I have bought new clothes
Is there a chance do you suppose,
That they'll no longer snub their nose
These fair and lovely ladies?

For often in the past perchance
When I would ask them for a dance.
They'd say, "You haven't got a chance".
These fair and lovely ladies.

Then I became a millionaire.
For once I didn't have a care.
I'd throw my money in the air
For these fair and lovely ladies.

I have found since I earned my fame
That life is quite a different game.
They think they've changed but they're' still the same
Those shallow lovely ladies.

For since ~ each one of them has said,
"Kind sir, please take me to your bed".
I smile and sadly shake my head
To these lonely lovely ladies.

I've found myself a lovely lad.
He makes me smile and I'm awfully glad
I no longer want the things they had,
From those sad and tawdry ladies.

The New Me

I'm Jim and not James
Now we are all changing names,
My decision is that's who I'll be.
For everyone here
Is making it clear
We must all chose *our* identity.
Now that we all have left home
And decided to room,
Although roaming is not what we do.
In setting us free ,
We'll decide what we'll be
And who we will also be too.
It's much better by far
Just to be who we are.
Allowed to do the things that we do.
We will not play your game.
We will chose our own name,
And not one that's given by you.
So dear mater and pater
When I speak to you later,
I trust you will not take offence.
For you did set me free
And I am sure you can see
It is all just plain commonsense.
So if you will quote
My new name from this note
The next time we're in conversation,
I think you'll agree
That between you and me,

Barney S. Smith

The new me cont...

We will have a more open relation.
So it's goodbye from me
And it's goodbye from him
And it's good just to make it all clear.
I'm not James, I am Jim,
And it's goodbye from him.
I just end with I love you all dear.

Childman

When does a child become a man,
When his parents tell him so?
And what if the parents get it wrong
Don't know when it's time to let go.

If so ~ what then happens to the man
Does he remain a child?
Unbridled and untamed feelings
Might tend to make him wild.

He could remain subservient
Having always been told no.
Left with no imagination
Not knowing how to grow.

Who then becomes responsible
For the child like un-grown man?
Lost in a world he does not know,
One he fails to understand.

His feelings tell him this is right.
Society says it's wrong
You should not be here!, but locked up.
Here is where you don't belong.

Mixed messages from all around.
Who is there to believe?
Just hide behind a vacant look
It's the best way to deceive.

And if by chance he is fortunate
To have children of his own;
Who'll be there to tell them right
So they won't grow like he has grown?

Barney S. Smith

Learning To Fly

A silent observer, in the ways of the world
I watched, as the banner of freedom unfurled.
I had no ticket to ride on a 'plane
But that spiritual journey will always remain.
For anyone watching, they truly were there.
The night Paul McCartney sang in Red Square.

The old ones, the young ones, they laughed and they cried
All swept along on an emotional tide.
Humanity carried away by a star
When he sang, 'I am Back In The USSR'.
Just twice in a life time freedom had come
In song they united, their bondage undone.

For the rest of a life time those there will say,
'When the call came for freedom, I was with them that day'.
Gone was oppression, no use was the gun
For the passion of living was with everyone.
Our hearts and our minds and our souls were laid bare.
The night Paul McCartney sang in Red Square.

All's Well

I'm a hypochondriac.
It started with my back
And then it spread to other places too.
It's a funny kind of feeling
When you're dizzy and you're reeling
And you are having trouble sitting on the loo.

For a long time I've been fearing
That I'm going to lose my hearing
I've already lost so many other things.
I now search everywhere
Just to find a single hair,
And I know my voice is breaking when I sing.

My belly has gone to pot
And my teeth ache such a lot.
I know that I've got trouble with my heart.
And both my feet are flat
And what's much worse than that
My knees knock when my legs are spread apart.

I often want to cry
When I look at my one eye
It would be as well if both of them were glass.
My breath is bad as well
It's an awful kind of smell.
But it might be better if we let that pass!

If you read this you might think
I'm a moaning kind of gink
But that's left to you, for only you can tell.
For when I'm sound asleep,
No one ever hears a peep
So I'll leave you now and hope you all **Keep Well.**

Barney S. Smith

Morning Gift

There is a soft and gentle stillness
In the early autumn morn.
Natures hint of her intention
For the world when it was born.

Field and hedgerow shimmering, sparkling,
Festooned with their ripened feast.
Offering gifts of tasty morsel
To tempt the birds and passing beast.

Night times cloak of darkness lifted.
Morning sheds its muted light
Revealing unseen track and pathway,
Earlier hidden by the night.

Nocturnal creatures now retired
To sleep away the daylight hours.
Flora meanwhile soft awakening
To share the glory of its flowers.

Lofty trees are now disrobing
Strewing their burnished leaves around,
Creating kaleidoscopes of colour.
Weaving a carpet on the ground.

The air is turning cooler daily.
Summer birds have long since gone.
The soaring lark no longer singing.
Silent is the thrushes song.

Morning gift cont...

A quiet time now harvest's ended.
And young can forage on their own.
Time to relax, time for reflection,
Time to note how the world has grown.

The earth is cool now to the touching;
The sky a different shade of blue.
And all is well with gods' creation.
A changing life forever new.

Who Dares

I wanted to purchase cloud Seven
Although the price was way over my head,
But someone had got there before me
So I settled for heaven instead.

For heaven was what you had shown me.
Your loving had pointed the way.
The light in your eye was the beacon,
And your smile just begged me to stay.

I am no more the wandering rover,
That ceased when you came along.
Now my rambling days are all over
For the love knot we tied is too strong.

The dreams I dream now, are real ones.
No more castles built in the air.
You can have every wish that you've wanted;
It's just grab hold, and win when you dare.

Had I not missed out on cloud Seven.
I would not be able to say,
That there are castles, there's clouds, and there's heaven.
Which one do you want? You just say.

For Your Eyes Only

I ached for your body to be there beside me
Holding me warm and close by your side.
To feel your strong arms wrapped gently around me,
But I was alone, the day that I died.

No sense of foreboding when I had awakened,
Nothing to say this would be my last day.
Only the letter you had left on your pillow.
You no longer loved me, you were leaving today.

A grey confused sense of panic invaded,
I fought to retain a sane sense of mind.
Try as I might, the thoughts still pervaded.
All was confusion - nothing defined.

Like a run-away robot, all control had departed;
A gyrating dervish locked into my head.
Yet no movement or sound escaped from my body
As I lay there, so wounded, alone in my bed.

From numbness to pain, to anger and reason,
I replayed the time of our life in my head.
When did the time of betrayal and treason
Enter your thoughts, to leave me for dead.

You had offered no sign of your chosen intention.
Or with my need of your love, I was too blind to see.
Now there's nobody here to make intervention
And I have chosen to die, so that you can be free.

The bottles are empty, no drink and no tablets.
My thoughts are still with you as I say farewell;
I can no longer suffer my torture in this world,
So my dearest beloved I will see you in hell.

Barney S. Smith

Band of Joy

I was visited by friends last night as I listened to some music.
They had n't been around for quite a while.
Just sharing time again with them made me sad, but happy,
For I rarely think of them without a smile.

Derek really loves brass bands ~ but then again does Giff
'Though they enjoy them in a different kind of way.
Derek plays euphonium with the Sally Army band
But I must confess, I have never heard him play.

Giff is more a marching man ~ military and proud
With a twirling mace that he throws to the sky.
No break in stride he catches it, then throws it up again.
I have never seen another go so high.

It's good that all the three of us have brass bands in common.
I listen ~ Giff conducts ~ and Derek play.
And the rapture of their music transports us all to heaven,
They would not have it any other way.

The strange thing is, the two of them have never ever met.
I mean not in the usual kind of way.
Of course they have in spirit, that's the most uplifting thing
And they do that when they hear a brass band play.

From somewhere up in heaven, they look down at me and smile
And I know that when they hear the angels sing.
They will be thinking of the next time when we will meet again,
For a brass band always means re-visiting.

To Be Loved

To love and be loved.
Who can explain
The exquisite pleasure
Of being insane?

To float down the street
On the heads of the crowd.
To draw their attention
By shouting out loud.

"You think I'm a fool.
Well! fool I may be
But are there any among you
As lucky as me?"

I can jump through a hoop,
I can run through the fire,
I can do any thing
That my heart might desire.

I can stand on the brink
I can bay at the moon
And not care a fig
That you think me a loon.

For something has happened
Just what I can't say,
For I'm now afflicted
In a wonderful way.

My advice to you, try it
And very soon you will see.
You'll be sharing the magic
With the world - just like me.

Barney S. Smith

Lovers Or?

For the husband, a mistress, for the wife a lover.
Each hoping that neither will discover
The secrets that they try to keep,
That pleasures or haunts them in their sleep.

Stolen fruits, so bitter sweet,
Are always with them when they meet.
Having to leave when you want to stay
But afraid that you're missed while you are away.

A wistful smile may light the face
But it isn't the time and it isn't the place.
Why don't they go out and leave me alone?
When they are here it's too risky to phone.

You are out with your spouse and how will you greet
When you are facing your lover out in the street?
Do you smile and then greet them, is that O.K.
Or pretend not to see them and just turn away?

Why do they do it? Is it love or for fun?
And how can they be sure that this is the one;
For sooner or later there will be a goodbye
Leaving a spouse, or a lover, with a tear in their eye.

So won't you consider before you embark
On something that starts for a bit of a lark?
For a passionate fling by a man, or his wife,
Could end up with someone taking their life.

Eaves Dropping

"What a lovely day," said the brightly plumed jay
As he glided away on the wing.
"Oh yes I agree," said the owl in the tree,
As the tiny wren started to sing.

The poor jilted robin was quietly sobbing
While all the great tits gathered round.
And the grey turtle dove, just hovered above
With his gaze firmly fixed on the ground.

"Oh you poor little chap," said his friend the blackcap.
"How could anyone do this to you?"
"Well he is rather mean", said the finch that was green.
"I agree said the tit that was blue".

"Don't be absurd," said the haughty blackbird.
"You have only your own self to blame".
"Ah, don't worry darling," said the speckled gay starling.
"Just go and play them at their own game".

The well dressed magpie looked him straight in the eye
And said ~ "Now don't give an inch".
"If you stay brave and bold, I will give you some gold"
Said the aristocratic goldfinch.

The pert yellowhammer then said, with a stammer,
"Bbut wwhat happened wwas not very nice."
The sparrow replied, as he took her aside,
"We've all done that at least once or twice."

Barney S. Smith

Eaves dropping cont...

"You are just a home wrecker," said the spotted woodpecker,
As he sharpened his beak on some bark.
The dunnock then twittered, "You are really dim witted."
It was only said for a lark.

Said the poor maiden thrush, with a bit of a blush,
" Oh dear what a terrible to do."
The redwing, with a sigh, gave her the eye.
Which said plainly, "I will will you."

The rook and the crow just didn't know,
The raven had seen it before.
"It's rather quite nice if it's twice more than thrice."
Smiled the promiscuously active jackdaw.

The visiting whitethroat in a falsetto note,
Said, "I have heard what you've all got to say."
"Cut out all the talk," Screeched the fierce sparrow hawk,
"It is time we went on our way."

The chaffinch and bullfinch just looked at each other
They agreed that was what they would do.
And the little goldcrest said, "Goodbye", to the rest.
And the lot of them flew away too.

Only Fools And Horses

I really did feel quite hungry
I could readily have eaten a horse.
But when I put that to him
He only said," Neigh" of course.

"How can I appease my hunger?"
I asked of this noble steed.
He replied, "Just grab a nosebag,
I'll let you have some of my feed."

My gaze must have been non - committal.
Even more ~ a look of forlorn.
For he tossed up his head and he snorted,
"If you don't like the feed try some corn."

By now I'm perplexed and I'm puzzled,
His snorting's filled me with alarm.
But he just trotted over and nuzzled
His great hairy head on my arm.

I'll admit I felt rather a coward
As he gently allayed all my fear.
He then moved his head to my shoulder
And bit a bloody great chunk, from my ear!

Barney S. Smith

Penance

I think I'll start detoxification.
Well I would if I knew what it meant.
Yes, I will start detoxification.
'Cause you've got to do something for lent.

No more chocs, no more fags, no more drinking.
Well I'll give up one of each every day.
Well at least that is what I am thinking
I will soon get much fitter that way.

With less chocs and less sweets I'll grow thinner
And my clothes will not fit anymore,
And I won't have pudding for dinner,
Well I never had it before.

No more fags ~ that might mean withdrawal,
I also could lose my bad breath
And with a *promise* I may make before all,
It could possibly save me from death.

No more drinking? Who ever does that one?
No more spirits, no beer and no wine.
Though I am assured by all those who do it
That living without drink, is just fine.

Yes I will start detoxification,
No more fags, no more sweets, no more beer.
As I see in my imagination
How you will all see me next year.

I'll be slimmer and fitter ~ more sprightly.
I will be also more active as well.
And I will tell all who ask ~ quite politely
That to go through all that, *is sheer* hell.

Happy Holidays

Here we are again
sitting on a plane.
First we are off to Palma,
a satellite of Spain.
Then to Monte Carlo,
a rich mans paradise.
With casino's and a harbour
it is very, very nice.
Then onward to Tunisia
a strange and mystic land.
Where the camels
always have the hump
because there's too much sand.
Next it's Citivechia
once visited by Caesar.
From there,
you might go on to Rome
or the leaning Tower of Pisa.
One more call,
the best of all,
the city of Barcelona.
Where the Spaniards flock
for their sticks of rock
or a flavoured ice cream cona.
Then back to Palma
for the air flight homeward bound.
A better type of holiday
I have never ever found.

Barney S. Smith

Home Town

Shabby homes, back street shambles
Every building old and worn.
What chance in life for those who live here?
Small hope if this is where you're born.

Concrete and weeds the only gardens,
No open fields for kids to play.
Just derelict buildings and broken fences;
Everywhere screams out decay.

The strain of life shows on the faces.
No sign of hope, just plain despair.
But only they may challenge and question,
No stranger asks "Why?" for no one dare.

Yet there is warmth for those who live there.
Their community's heart beat as just one.
What other hope is there, there for them?
But one for all!, and all for one!

Few have tried the break for freedom,
None have made it, that is why.
And the fear of ostricisation
Is the only reward if you should try.

So they stay within their confines
For in their heart each one will know,
This is where they'll end their living.
There is no other place to go.

Gifted

He sat all alone in the corner
His hands placed firm on his head.
Nobody paid him attention
"I didn't do it", he said.

Tears welled in his eyes as he sat there
Bewildered, alone, and head bowed.
Would somebody please re-assure him?
But he hadn't a friend in the crowd.

His small shoulders hunched as he sat there
His body moved close to the ground.
He still was n't sure what was taken,
Just prayed that it soon would be found.

Why was it that no one believed him?
He sat there just shaking his head.
So what if he lived alone with his mother.
Didn't they know that his father was dead?

What if they were poor, often cold, often hungry
And the clothes that they wore were not new?
They were clean, they were proud and they were faithful,
And always did what was given to do.

An awareness of someone beside him
Smart shoes of an elderly gent.
With startled surprise, he saw two gentle blue eyes
Looking down with the deepest intent.

The old man placed a hand on the boy's shoulder
And gently ruffled his hair.
He said, "At last my seeking is over,
For I have searched for you everywhere."

Barney S. Smith

Gifted cont...

"I have just had a word with your mother,
When I saw her I knew she was the one
Who had tended and cared for my most precious gift,
And who married my runaway son.
So you see, you are really my grandson.
The reason my son ran away
Your parents thought I could never forgive them
But I had, from the very first day."

The boy shook his head as he mumbled,
"They all say I have done something bad.
So I too will now have to leave you
And run away just like my dad."

The old man squeezed the little lad's shoulder
Again fondling the hair on his head.
"It has been far too long, and you've done nothing wrong
I am taking you both to my home", he said.

"It seems that whatever was missing
Has never been here at all.
The delivery was meant for today
But they haven't had time to call."

No longer blamed and a lost sense of shame
Seemed to set the little boy free.
With a now smiling face, he left that sad place
And went off with his new found family.

I Caught A Feeling

I caught a feeling this morning,
And took a peep inside.
I held it firm and gently
For it had no where to hide.

It had this rare expression,
A picture of my life.
Of piety and gaiety,
Of sadness and of strife.

The emotions held inside me
All rolled into one.
Love, and hate, and gentleness,
Misery and fun.

It showed me what I carried,
From a very tender age
The things I've held inside me
Like passion, fear and rage.

It showed me joy and jollity,
Excitement and delight,
It held the warmth of sunshine
And the coolness of the night.

To feel glad that I am living,
To wonder at each new day.
Yes, I caught a feeling this morning,
And I pray that it will stay.

Barney S. Smith

Silver Day

A river runs through like a silver thread
That carries the meaning of life.
Like loving, and caring, and wondrous things,
That a man may share with a wife.

For rivers can rage or be gentle and calm.
Just like marriage, as most of us know.
It is then faith in a partner, or faith in a love,
Helps us manage to go with the flow.

For love is a treasure that cannot be bought.
It's a prize that can only be given.
And the meaning of life is that which is sought
In this gift that was fashioned in heaven.

It's a gift to be nurtured and tended with care,
With sadness, and laughter, and tears,
And the things that can happen when two people share
Life together for twenty-five years.

For two special people, for Chris and for Don,
May the journey continue to be.
The one they deserve for just who they are,
That, which I hope they continue to be.

"Hello"

Now there is leisure time
So much more pleasure time
From when we first said,
"Hello"

Those dreams way from the past
Oh how we made them last
We brought them back from time
To make this life sublime
So we could just say,
"Hello"

I have the memory when
You first smiled at me
It's in my treasury
That first, "Hello"

Those days back in the sun
When life and love were fun
I have them with me still
I guess I always will
That warm embracing first,
"Hello"

And now our closing days
Remind me in many ways
That life is still out there
And if you want your share
Well just smile and say again
Your first, "Hello"

Oh Mind Be Still

Oh mind be still
And find the peace your seeking.
Embrace the calm
That's offered with each new day.
Take strength from all
The words your heart is speaking.
In them be sure ,
That love will find a way.

Open your eyes
To all the gifts around you.
Open your mind
To all the inner things you see.
Be sure to find
The bounties that surround you.
The wondrous gifts of nature,
Offered free.

Why stain the great book
With tears when there is no need too.
Love can enter
The places tears cannot go.
Hearts may be wounded,
broken, bleeding.
Love is the balm
That gently ease the flow.

Love is the strength,
That binds our lives together.
Faith is the vision
That illuminates the way.
Hope is entwined
In every new decision .
Life is proclaimed
With every word we say..

Stony Cold

Look into my eyes and tell me that you love me.
Tell me dear that we've not grown apart.
Tell me there's no room for any other,
Only room for me within your heart.

Say anything my love but don't ignore me,
I beg you please don't treat me like a child.
Hold me to your heart just press me to you
Until my quaking fears are reconciled.

All my life you know that I've adored you.
Making dreams for us when we grow old.
But in return scorn's all that I get back from you,
In that dismissive look so stony cold.

I know I can no longer live without you.
To share with you this life of discontent.
You know I've tried so hard to never doubt you,
But now my strength and patience is all spent.

So my darling it is time for me to leave you.
There's nothing more that I can do or say.
So little time now left for me to grieve you,
As my dying breath and life blood flows away.

Another Dollar

Another day another dollar
That's what you'll hear them say,
If you ever have the time
To visit the U.S. of A.

But who's it for and what's it for
To purchase a few more things.
Another burden for your back
Each time the cash till rings.

"Good morning madam", "Can I help you sir"
They ask with their sickly grin
But then they are only doing their best
To make the cash tills ring.

"The hat looks nice it matches the dress"
(He hates the beastly thing)
No matter that she looks a mess
As he hears the cash till ring.

"Are Sir, you are taking the shirt then with the suit"
His heart begins to sing.
Commission signs light up his eyes
As again the cash till ring.

His feet are sore, the doors are closed.
No one knows what pleasure this bring,
For now he can sit and gloat on the loot
That made the cash tills ring.

Open Mind

Close your eyes and open your mind
Just relax and you will find,
As shapes and colours are quickly unfurled,
You are entering into another world.

Colours and shapes you have not before seen,
And places where you have never been.
Ogliepoid worglies, and stroogers, and squiggers,
Small teeny weenies, and bigger than biggers.

These amazing creatures can appear,
There will be some that you love and some that you fear.
Some to let go of and some to hold
Some of them gems more precious than gold.

A soft misty vista a stark craggy feature.
A fairy or ghoul or some other creature.
So open your mind and just close your eyes,
You could find yourself in for a wondrous surprise.

To Be

Stay awhile and let us reminisce
Of other days and other times we've shared like this.
For memories and life are in the sharing,
And life and friendship's good within the daring.

Of expressing thoughts of cherished hopes and hidden fears.
Of sharing in the moment of laughter and the pain of tears.
The knowing and the growing in the friendship deal
Recognition but acceptance in the way we feel.

Holding and being held without the touching.
Learning to let go without the need for clutching.
Showing strength without the need for posing
Allowing closure when there is a need for closing.

Appreciating silence when there is a need for space.
Recognising spirituality and the power of 'grace'.
And when there is no need for words but just the sign
Your understanding of the moment is the same as mine.

These are the precious times when being is just to be.
Those very special times,
When I am very close to you,
And you are close to me.

READERS NOTES

READERS NOTES

READERS NOTES